IMAGES
of America

EAST HARTFORD

On June 17, 1928, many town residents attended the unveiling of the Rochambeau monument on Silver Lane adjacent to Silver Lane School, where it remains to this day. The East Hartford High School glee club sang "La Marseillaise" in French, and a parade commemorated the event. The Comte de Rochambeau and his 5,000 French troops, who helped Americans during the Revolutionary War, encamped on Silver Lane in 1781 on their way to help Gen. George Washington and again in 1782 on their return march.

On the cover: Please see above. (Roy Spiller collection.)

IMAGES
of America

EAST HARTFORD

East Hartford Rotary Club
with Raymond Johnson

ARCADIA
PUBLISHING

Published by Arcadia Publishing
Charleston, South Carolina

Library of Congress Control Number: 2008940760

For all general information contact Arcadia Publishing at:
Telephone 843-853-2070
Fax 843-853-0044
E-mail sales@arcadiapublishing.com
For customer service and orders:
Toll-Free 1-888-313-2665

Visit us on the Internet at www.arcadiapublishing.com

CONTENTS

ACKNOWLEDGMENTS

Ray Johnson is a past president of the East Hartford Historical Society. He was a teacher in the town's school system for 35 years and wrote the school district's curriculum on the history of East Hartford. Listed in *Who's Who in American Education,* Ray is a recipient of the Milken National Educator Award and the Jaycee's Outstanding Teacher Award.

To help celebrate the East Hartford Rotary Club's 80th anniversary, members resolved to publish an Images of America book about the town's rich historical past. Joining the author were three Rotarians who donated many hours to this project. Without their help the book could not have been brought to completion: Jackie Danise contributed her organizational, research, and typing skills; Bill Secord contributed his knowledge of photography, computer technology, and grammar; and Roy Spiller contributed his knowledge of the town's history, his extensive photography collection, and his high level of energy and enthusiasm.

The Rotary Club of East Hartford, established in 1928, is a member of Rotary International, a worldwide organization of Rotary clubs committed to the motto "Service Above Self." East Hartford Rotary supports many town-focused charitable programs, particularly educational and scholarship programs; and it participates in international projects such as the eradication of polio.

The author and the East Hartford Rotary Club thank the many residents of town who contributed pictures and historical information. They also extend thanks to the staff of the Raymond Library and the Thomas J. Dodd Research Center at the University of Connecticut.

INTRODUCTION

East Hartford's present 11,000 acres were once the home of a tribe of timid Native Americans known as the Podunks. The Connecticut River and its rich fertile plain provided an abundant food supply, while moose, deer, and beaver skins assured warmth for the cold winters. Wigwam-type structures provided shelter. They were built along the Connecticut River during the summer and moved farther east to other parts of the town in the fall for greater warmth. Podunk Indians were peace loving and fought only when other marauding tribes threatened their terrain.

The sachem, or chief, of the Podunks realized a real threat from the Pequot Indians who had periodically attacked the East Hartford tribe, and he thought the settling of white men in the area might deter the attacks. In 1631, Wahginnacut ventured to Boston to speak with Puritan leaders and attempt to convince them of the benefits of life on the east bank of the Connecticut River. He offered beaver skins, free land, and seeds for crops. The Puritans, however, were uninterested at the time. Later they would come in such large numbers that the Podunk Indians could not maintain their lifestyle, and the tribe would cease to exist by the middle of the next century.

Farming of the rich East Hartford land was done mainly by the female members of the tribe, while the men daily hunted or fished. Crops of maize, beans, squash, and pumpkins were cultivated and incorporated into many dishes that are still today served in homes throughout town. Succotash and pumpkin pie were treats to the Podunks, as they are to contemporary residents. Cooking utensils consisted of crudely made clay pots, which children helped to fashion. The cooking of meat and fish was done on sticks or in large holes dug in the ground and lined with rocks to hold the heat. As late summer approached, a cache of smoked fish and meat would be stored for the long winter, when the only hope of fresh meat would be squirrels or deer.

Winter brought the dismantling of wigwams along the river and their rebuilding farther inland. If a family was too large for a wigwam, lodges measuring approximately 25 feet by 12 feet were constructed from wood, skins, and bark. Both types of structure contained a stone fireplace located in the center on the dirt floor with a hole in the roof above to act as a chimney. The fireplace served solely as a means for cooking, as numerous layers of skins and furs were used for body warmth.

With the advent of Dutch and English settlers to the area, the Podunks gradually died off or moved away. Two heavily traveled roads today, however, are laid out along the original Podunk trails. As cars travel quickly over Main Street and Tolland Street, very few people realize that these very routes were in heavy use by the Podunks 400 years ago.

The first white settler in East Hartford was John Crow, who moved here from Hartford in 1639. By 1640, the first road in town was laid out along what is now Prospect Street. William Goodwin soon followed Crow; and in 1654, he built the first sawmill on the Hockanum River, then called the Saw Mill River. Settlers thronged to Goodwin's mill to cut lumber for homes. As the number of settlers increased, other mills opened, including gristmills to grind grain into flour.

In the late 1600s, the most notable William Pitkin moved to East Hartford. His family would play a major role in both town and state affairs for centuries to come, and the Pitkin name has survived and prospered into this century.

By 1699, East Hartford had become a separate parish from Hartford because town residents had complained bitterly about the need to cross the river for Sunday worship services. This new status allowed town residents the right to tax land for schools and churches. The first meetinghouse for East Hartford residents was built at this time on the corner of Main and Pitkin Streets. The dominant form of religion was Congregationalism, derived from Puritanism.

As the 17th century ended, most citizens of East Hartford lived near the present center of town; however, families were spreading to the forested areas as more land grants were issued from England or as earlier residents sold parcels of land. Two homes that were very isolated when constructed are today part of built-up neighborhoods—the Keeney homestead on Forbes Street and the Porter homestead on Maple Street. When the massacre at Deerfield, Massachusetts, took place in 1704, homes such as these were fortified with large fences, as residents feared a similar attack here.

During the early 1700s, East Hartford prospered with its numerous mills and fertile lands. Most residents were proud of their town and were also loyal British subjects. The flag that flew on special occasions was the British Union Jack, and goods were sold in pounds instead of dollars. The year 1731 saw Benjamin Hills sell part of lower Silver Lane to the town, thus opening up this area for development. Many present-day homes on Silver Lane near Main Street date from this period. Also during this period, Levi Goodwin opened a tavern in the northern portion of East Hartford near the present intersection of Main Street and Ellington Road. Goodwin's home remains; his tavern, however, which was adjacent to it, has long been gone. This tavern was a landmark in East Hartford during the mid-1700s and was a gathering place much like a modern English pub.

While slavery was not as common in the North as in the South, it did exist; in 1761, there were 23 African American slaves in East Hartford. Although little is known of their treatment, they were owned by such prominent families as the Williams, Goodwins, and Olmsteds.

The disagreements that led to the Revolutionary War were felt locally, and East Hartford was destined to play a vital role in the conflict. William Pitkin of East Hartford, grandson of the William Pitkin who was one of the town's first settlers, was elected to the governorship of Connecticut in 1766. Firmly believing in separation from England, Governor Pitkin became a convincing voice to other lawmakers who at first did not share his views.

East Hartford was well equipped with growing industries and staunch supporters for independence. When news came about Lexington and Concord in 1775, many town residents walked to Massachusetts to join what would become a long war. Francis Hanmer, Charles Forbes, and George Pitkin owned two powder mills along the Hockanum River; at the beginning of the war, these two mills became the major suppliers of gunpowder for George Washington's army. Another member of the Pitkin family, Joseph Pitkin, who had established an iron-making foundry in the 1750s, supplied guns to the Continental army.

In 1775, George Green, editor of the *Connecticut (Hartford) Courant*, established the first paper mill in town in order for his newspaper to have a ready supply of newsprint. The war, however, again took priority; the mill turned out a large portion of the writing paper used by officers in the Continental army.

The community strongly supported the revolution and voiced deep hatred toward the British. In 1777, town selectmen voted not to allow British prisoners of war to be jailed in East Hartford. Neighboring South Windsor had to make provisions for them after this date.

The highlight of the Revolutionary War period for East Hartford residents occurred in the summer of 1781 when Comte de Rochambeau and 5,000 members of his French army marched into East Hartford and encamped there for four days. Elated about the French help during the war, the townspeople gave the blue-and-white-clad soldiers a tumultuous welcome. Most of the French were encamped along Silver Lane and in public houses along Main Street. A hospital was set up nearby. Town residents cooked large feasts and treated the soldiers royally. Activities were planned for each day, and dances were held each evening. As the French troops left East Hartford to attack the British in New York, both soldiers and residents were sad to see the festivities and friendships end.

During this encampment de Rochambeau's troops were paid in silver, a rare metal to Americans during the revolution. Legend has it that residents thereafter called this road Silver Lane because of all the silver coins that had been seen there. Many townspeople today believe this explanation, but some historians feel the street actually received its name from a silversmith who lived there earlier. No proof exists for either story, and the mystery persists.

At the conclusion of the Revolutionary War, East Hartford again petitioned for official separation from Hartford, and the Connecticut General Assembly awarded the town its own charter in 1783.

By the year 1800, East Hartford was in the front rank of American industry. Papermaking was substantial along the Hockanum River. Powder mills, cotton and woolen mills, sawmills, and gristmills dotted the town. Farming, however, was still the main way to earn a living, and tobacco was rapidly becoming the leading crop. While most East Hartford residents at this time were of British extraction, a large number of Scottish workers were settling in the Burnside area, which was once called Scotland. Today Scotland Road attests to their former presence.

A dramatic change came to East Hartford in 1849 with the construction of the Providence and Fishkill Railroad. East Hartford was destined to soon become a railroad center. A large number of Irish immigrants came to town to help construct the railroad, and shortly thereafter the town's first Catholic parish was established.

Throughout the 19th century most East Hartford residents earned their income by tobacco farming, working for the railroad, or laboring in the papermaking mills. The end of the 19th century brought East Hartford the first town firehouses, the Raymond Library, and horse-drawn trolley cars, which allowed easier access to Hartford. The huge wooden covered bridge connecting these two towns burned in 1895, forcing East Hartford residents to again rely on the ferry until the present Bulkeley Bridge opened in 1908.

As East Hartford celebrated the arrival of the 20th century, few residents probably realized that this sleepy farm town would emerge as one of Hartford's most densely settled suburbs and an industrial center known around the world. In 1929, Pratt and Whitney Aircraft purchased huge amounts of acreage along Main Street for the construction of a plant to build aircraft engines. Coming at the beginning of the Depression, the plant was welcomed for both tax revenues and job opportunities. During the 1930s, the company made steady growth and became a major town taxpayer.

Also during this era, the town experienced two major natural disasters that would later dictate much of the town's land use. In 1936, the Connecticut River overflowed its banks and covered one third of the town. In 1938, another major flood occurred because of the Great New England Hurricane. The Army Corps of Engineers then determined the need to construct the present dikes, which have successfully prevented the reoccurrence of flooding disasters.

At the end of the 1930s and the beginning of the 1940s, Pratt and Whitney became an extremely busy place as hostilities mushroomed into World War II. Workers came from all over New England, resulting in a severe housing shortage. Town officials and Pratt and Whitney Aircraft begged residents to rent out spare rooms. Mayberry Village was built in 1942 to alleviate some of the problem. Temporary housing units that looked like barracks dotted the town but have since been torn down. Millbrook Park was constructed as owner-occupied homes selling for $3,800—$380 down and $38 per month. The housing crunch during World War II was never fully addressed at the time, and the postwar years saw a major building boom. Most workers who came here from other areas liked the community and decided to stay. By 1949, East Hartford was the fastest-growing town east of the Mississippi River.

The 1950s saw continuing population growth and major building programs. Most schools were overcrowded and on double sessions until new buildings took care of the situation. By the 1960s, a second high school was built. Through the end of the 20th century East Hartford continued to grow but at a slower pace as the town's available land was used up.

The town continued to evolve as it entered the 21st century. Rentschler Field, once a bustling airfield for Pratt and Whitney, became home to the University of Connecticut football stadium. Tailgaters have replaced airplanes, and on days when games are played, fans from all over the state uproariously cheer their favorite team. Nearby a newly constructed Cabela's outlet, the first in New England, draws huge crowds from throughout the Northeast. Excitement regarding plans for future development at Rentschler Field extends to a building boom along the riverfront. Goodwin College is extensively expanding its facilities on a beautiful campus along the scenic Connecticut River. Main Street is also experiencing a rebirth with new structures complementing the historic buildings nearby. An attractive fountain now sits on the corner of Main Street and Connecticut Boulevard to welcome all to the center of town, and a gazebo built by the Rotary Club enhances a new town green.

While many residents of other communities view East Hartford as an industrial town, almost 50,000 people proudly call it home. Despite its size, East Hartford fosters a strong sense of local community. With pride in the town's heritage, its residents look forward to a future as bright as its past.

One

HERE LIE OUR ROOTS

Wells Tavern, a relic of the Revolutionary War era, was once located on the northeast corner of Main Street and Wells Avenue. It was a well-known stagecoach stop and featured a spacious barroom and low-ceilinged hall for dancing parties. While most overnight guests experienced spartan sleeping chambers, one chamber was reserved for special guests. It had flowery blue wallpaper, a fireplace, and two high-posted canopy beds. When Pres. James Monroe stayed at Wells Tavern in 1817, he undoubtedly was accommodated in this special room. (Roy Spiller collection.)

THE SECOND MEETING HOUSE, 1740—1835,
DRAWN BY HARRY D. OLMSTED FROM DESCRIPTIONS GIVEN BY THE FEW WHO REMEMBER IT.

The Second Meeting House is shown in a drawing done by Henry D. Olmsted in 1902. It was located approximately near the present-day corner of Pitkin and Main Streets. The two-story building had an elevated pulpit on the west side of the building with a large sounding board above it. The best seats were given to parishioners who contributed the most and also to those of advanced years. (Roy Spiller collection.)

The First Congregational Church on Main Street is East Hartford's oldest established church. The present structure was constructed in 1835. It was preceded by two other structures, the first constructed in 1699. The second building was begun in 1740, and some of the wood from that structure is in the present building. This beautiful Greek Revival building originally cost $9,309 to construct. The Town of East Hartford paid $1,000 for the right to use the basement for town meetings, a practice it followed for nearly 50 years. (Roy Spiller collection.)

12

The Pitkin family mill used the power of the Hockanum River to manufacture gunpowder. One of the first mills in the colonies to manufacture gunpowder, it supplied powder to the Continental army during the Revolutionary War. (Roy Spiller collection.)

Levi Goodwin, a mid-18th-century East Hartford tobacco farmer, built this home for his wife and family of five children in 1750. Along with farming, he ran a successful tavern, which was located behind his Main Street home facing King's Highway (present-day Ellington Road). Goodwin headed for Massachusetts to join the Continental army during the Revolutionary War, leaving the maintenance of the farm and tavern to his wife and children. At the conclusion of the war, Goodwin returned and held a huge three-day celebration at his tavern. (Photograph by Bill Secord.)

The Squire Elisha Pitkin home, shown in the distance, was once located near the corner of Main and Pitkin Streets. This pastoral scene greatly contrasts to present-day Pitkin Street with its many businesses and heavy traffic. (Raymond Library collection.)

The rear portion of the Squire Elisha Pitkin House was built prior to 1740, the main house being constructed in the early 1800s. It was deeded to the town in 1941 with the intent that it would be restored. Unfortunately, this restoration did not occur, and the house reverted back to the Pitkin heirs, who had it dismantled and moved to Guilford in 1952. (Roy Spiller collection.)

In 1781, 5,000 French soldiers under the command of Comte de Rochambeau made camp along Silver Lane on their march from Rhode Island to join Gen. George Washington in New York. In 1782, they marched from Yorktown, Virginia, back to Rhode Island and again encamped along Silver Lane. This home, now long gone, is believed to have been used as the quartermaster's headquarters, where he paid the French soldiers in silver that had been shipped up the Connecticut River. (Ray Johnson collection.)

The Huguenot House was built in 1761 by Edmund Bemont after he purchased two and a half acres along Country Road, now known as Burnside Avenue. The home was built on speculation and sold. Four years later, Edmund's son Makens and his wife, Pamelia, bought the home. They raised their children there, and Makens ran a saddle maker's shop from the home. When the house faced demolition in 1971, townspeople generously contributed the funding necessary to move it to Martin Park and restore it to its original beauty. (East of the River Tourism District collection.)

The Elijah Hills House, built around 1810, is located at 641 Hills Street. It is a post-and-beam house with the frame made of hand-hewed chestnut and all connections made by wooden pegs. A small building once stood adjacent to the house and served as a store and post office for the southeastern section of town, known as Hillstown. Hillstown Grange No. 87 had its first meetings in what is now the dining room of the Elijah Hills House. (Photograph by Bill Secord.)

The town farm or almshouse was located at 62 High Street near the present-day Hockanum School. Built in 1823 with an addition added in 1849, the farm remained in existence until 1944. People down on their luck would be housed and cared for; others could be sentenced to go there for minor infractions or unpaid tax bills. The town farm was mostly self-sustaining, as crops were raised and harvested by those who resided there. (Robert Sukosky collection.)

The Selden Brewer Home, located on the corner of Naubuc Avenue and Main Street, was built between 1827 and 1833. According to family tradition, Selden's father Samuel brought the bricks for the home from Wethersfield in wagonloads over the frozen Connecticut River during the winter of 1827. The Brewer family is historically important to East Hartford because of its prominence in the tobacco-growing industry. (Ray Johnson collection.)

The building of octagon-shaped homes was a fad during the late 1840s–1860s. Eight-sided homes were thought to be easier to heat, provide more room and better circulation, and generally provide a more healthful environment. Gradually people found these things to be untrue, and the building of octagonal homes virtually ceased. Rev. Benjamin C. Phelps built this octagonal house on Naubuc Avenue in 1852 after serving as minister of the Hockanum Methodist Church for three years. (Photograph by Bill Secord.)

The building located where Church Street ends and Forbes Street begins is one of the nation's oldest sites still being operated as a mill. The building on the right, which still stands, dates from the Civil War era. For many years, it was home to the Dovalette Paper Company. During the 1950s and 1960s, radio station WTIC and the Dovalette Company sponsored a contest, and cars spotted with the Dovalette box on display won a prize. (Robert Sukosky collection.)

St. John's Episcopal Church on the corner of Main Street and Burnside Avenue was constructed between 1867 and 1869 in High Victorian Gothic style. Its architect was the well-known Edward Tuckerman Potter, who also designed Hartford's famous Mark Twain House. Potter visited the Far East prior to designing St. John's Episcopal Church, and the pagoda-like shape of the belfry and roof is indicative of the architect's fondness for the architecture he viewed on his trip. (Ray Johnson collection.)

18

MASONIC TEMPLE, EAST HARTFORD, CONN.

Edward Hayden originally owned the land where the present Masonic temple/Orient lodge is located. Hayden, a Civil War veteran, farmer, and teacher, sold the land to Albert C. Raymond in 1874. About this time, Raymond constructed this large Italianate home, where he and his wife would reside. Raymond is best known as the man who donated land and money for the present Raymond Library. A successful businessman and farmer, Raymond died with no natural heirs in 1880. (Ray Johnson collection.)

The Samuel Forbes house of 398 Silver Lane, a Second Empire home, was built in 1878. The two-and-a-half-story home boasts many notable features, including a diamond-paneled sash, reliefs surrounding windows and doors, and a slate roof. Samuel Forbes was a successful tobacco grower. His family lived the comfortable life of wealthy plantation owners and was very influential in town affairs. (Ray Johnson collection.)

For the last 100 years, East Hartford has had one newspaper, the *East Hartford Gazette*. For about 30 years beginning in 1888, it had two newspapers, the *Gazette* and the *American Enterprise*, published by James Martin. Martin's newspaper heavily favored the nationally active labor movement, and he included both national and international news in his editions. His beautiful Main Street home, pictured here, was recently destroyed by fire. (Ray Johnson collection.)

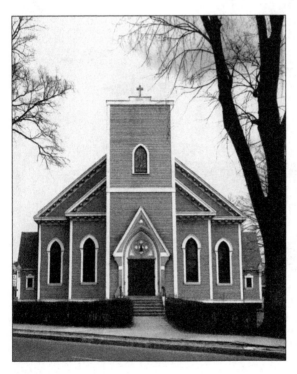

East Hartford's increasing Irish and Italian population in the 19th century created a need for the construction of the town's first Roman Catholic church. St. Mary's Church was built in 1877 on the corner of Woodbridge Avenue and Main Street. Its first pastor, Patrick Goodwin, was a native of Ireland. This photograph was taken after 1938, as St. Mary's lost its steeple in that year to the winds of the Great New England Hurricane. (Raymond Library collection.)

The early 20th century found beautiful elm trees lining Main Street before they succumbed to the Dutch elm disease that killed trees throughout the area. To the right is St. Mary's Church. Its steeple would be blown down in the 1938 hurricane. (Roy Spiller collection.)

The Hillstown Grange was the center of activity in the southeastern section of town during the late 1800s through the 1900s. Organized in 1888, it still functions as a Grange and has a large and active membership. Granges originally began to gather farmers together to support legislation and to provide needed insurance against storms and insects that damaged crops. The Grange also served as a social center for farmers and their families. The Hillstown Grange still sponsors numerous activities, including public dinners and an annual agricultural fair. (Photograph by Bill Secord.)

Dr. Edward W. Pratt (1863–1909) had his office at 765 Main Street at the corner of Garvan Street. During his years of practice, dentistry was far different from today. Anesthesia was a 19th-century invention, but for extractions laughing gas was most commonly used. Some 28 dental schools existed in the country, as dentistry became an accepted profession. (Roy Spiller collection.)

Due to Dr. Pratt's lucrative dentistry practice, his family lived a life of luxury in their Main Street home. Their house was ornately decorated, as was the custom of the time. (Roy Spiller collection.)

Dr. Pratt's office was state of the art for the 19th century. In the 1880s, the collapsible metal tube revolutionized toothpaste manufacturing. Before then, teeth-cleaning powders and liquids were made by dentists and sold to their patients. The first dental x-rays were used in the 1890s. (Roy Spiller collection.)

Dr. Thomas O'Connell, shown in front of his Burnside Avenue home, was about to begin his daily rounds of visiting patients. This highly respected and much-loved physician has both a street and a school in town named after him. His home near the corner of Elm Street is now a lawyer's office. (Ray Johnson collection.)

The W. X. Truesdale Company was located on Tolland Street. The building on the left was a storage shed, while the big building on the right was a store that sold flour, bran, and wholesale and retail seed. Painted on the side of the wagon is "Truesdale and Company, Burnside, Connecticut." (Robert Sukosky collection.)

Majestic elm trees lined much of Main Street in the 19th century. The center strip of trees would eventually be removed as electric trolleys were introduced and space was needed for tracks. (Raymond Library collection.)

The International Order of Odd Fellows building was located on Main Street near the corner of present-day Governor Street. This postcard shows the building's appearance at the beginning of the 20th century. The post office was also housed in this building and sold first-class postage stamps for 2¢ each. (Roy Spiller collection.)

Hartford Avenue, now called Connecticut Boulevard, was a far less traveled thoroughfare in the early 20th century. Then a primarily residential area, it is today home to a wide variety of offices and businesses. (Roy Spiller collection.)

This early-20th-century postcard showing the corner of Main Street and Burnside Avenue depicts a very placid scene, far different from the busy intersection that exists today. At the beginning of the 20th century most people traveled by horse, trolley, or bicycle. By 1915, Henry Ford would build his one millionth automobile, and East Hartford would rapidly change its mode of transportation along with the rest of the country. (Roy Spiller collection.)

The first residents of 21 Elm Street were the Styles family. Lucius Styles, his father, and his father's brother were all doctors. (Madore family collection.)

Connecticut Boulevard is today home to East Hartford's automobile row, where customers may choose to purchase a Smart Car or Rolls Royce, along with many other models. In the early 20th century, supplying automotive needs was far different, as this photograph indicates. (Roy Spiller collection.)

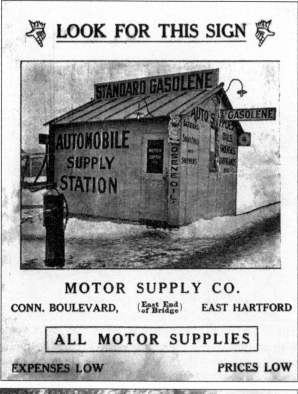

LOOK FOR THIS SIGN

MOTOR SUPPLY CO.

CONN. BOULEVARD,   (East End of Bridge)   EAST HARTFORD

ALL MOTOR SUPPLIES

EXPENSES LOW   PRICES LOW

Roy Clark, the self-proclaimed "Baby Chick Man" in a 1923 advertisement, operated his establishment at 15 Burnside Avenue. This photograph, which dates from the same year, shows his Ford Model T one-ton delivery truck. His advertisement also stated that Clark's chicks won the state laying contest and that two hatches occurred every week. (Roy Spiller collection.)

The Colonial Oil Company was one of East Hartford's largest suppliers in the early part of the 20th century, as this photograph of its fleet indicates. During this time, America met all of its petroleum needs domestically and provided almost 70 percent of the world's oil demands. The 1924 discovery of vast oil reserves in Texas, Oklahoma, and California would provide cheap fuel for much of the 20th century. (Roy Spiller collection.)

Bogue's General Store was located on the northeast corner of Silver Lane and Main Street, presently the site of Town Fair Tire Company. Later it was bought by the Johnson family and was operated under the name Silver Lane Grocery Store. It was one of many small stores throughout town that served local residents before chain supermarkets came to town. (Robert Sukosky collection.)

This photograph, taken in 1930 on Connecticut Boulevard, shows a Hartford Despatch truck. Founded in 1906 as the Springfield Hartford Express, the company moved to its new warehouse in East Hartford around 1920 and for many decades provided public warehousing and distribution services to companies such as First National Stores, General Electric, Pratt and Whitney, and many others. In 1928, Hartford Despatch became a charter member of Allied Van Lines. It continues to operate its public warehouse and household moving and storage business in the same location on Prospect Street. (Robert Sukosky collection.)

Kenneth G. Clark's Esso service station was located on the corner of Main and Orchard Streets. It was torn down to allow expansion of the First Federal Savings Bank building, which is currently owned by Goodwin College. (Roy Spiller collection.)

Downtown East Hartford around 1930 still shows some of the elm trees that once lined both sides and the center of the street. Trolley tracks came to town in 1889, horsecars arrived in 1890, and electric cars were running on tracks in 1892. Traffic certainly has increased since this photograph was taken. (Ray Johnson collection.)

This c. 1932 photograph shows Goba's gas station on the corner of Burnside Avenue and Mary Street, presently the site of Paul Buetner Florist. The small gas station was typical of the era. For many years, the Goba family also sold plants they raised in their Mary Street greenhouse. (G. William Miller collection.)

McKinley Brothers Gas Station was located across the street from the Raymond Library. Owner Sam McKinley's home is shown on the right. There was a restaurant in the middle of the building, the service station on the right, and Holland Atkins Flower Shop on the left. Today the building has been converted into a branch office of the Bank of America. (Roy Spiller collection.)

The thousands of defense workers at Pratt and Whitney during World War II created a severe housing shortage in town. Despite material shortages caused by the war, a new housing development called Millbrook Park was started in 1942. The homes sold out almost immediately. The Cape Cod–style homes required a $380 deposit and the monthly mortgage charge of $37.89. The very first home built was at 26 Oxford Drive and purchased by Mr. and Mrs. Herman Loman. Herman Loman was a Coast Guard inspector at the nearby Pratt and Whitney plant. This photograph shows how the house appears today. (Photograph by Bill Secord.)

Many high school students are waiting at the bus stop in front of the Eastwood Theater in this 1947 photograph. East Hartford's population that year was 30,000. There were 4,928 dwellings in town and 10,500 telephones with most people still sharing party lines. The average price of a home was $8,900, and the East Hartford Housing Authority was managing 1,356 rental units. Returning servicemen seeking housing swelled the housing authority's waiting list to 850. (Ray Johnson collection.)

Mayberry Village, named after a beloved town physician, was built in 1942 by the federal government to alleviate the housing shortage in town. Thousands of World War II defense workers from throughout the country moved to East Hartford to work at Pratt and Whitney, Hamilton Standard, and Chance Vought. At first, 500 homes were built on former farmland, and soon 150 more were constructed. (Raymond Library collection.)

Two

EARTH AND AIR

The Silver Lane Pickle Company was established by Frank Gould in the late 1800s. He built his first factory in the fertile fields along Silver Lane in 1902. The business thrived through the 1950s, and many town high school students found summer employment at the pickle factory. (Joan Maschi collection.)

PICKLES

SILVER LANE OF COURSE!

SILVER LANE PICKLE CO.

The smiling pickle trademark of the Silver Lane Pickle Company was known and respected throughout New England. The taste of their dill pickles was superb. Who could resist buying a jar that had such a happy-looking label? (Roy Spiller collection.)

Workers at the Silver Lane Pickle Company are processing a huge vat of sauerkraut in this 1940s photograph. A local resident fondly, or not so fondly, remembers his car being permeated with the smell of cabbage growing in the fields along Silver Lane. (Roy Spiller collection.)

Huge vats of pickling cucumbers were prepared daily at the Silver Lane Pickle Company. (Roy Spiller collection.)

In 1961, the Silver Lane Pickle Company was sold to the John E. Cain Company of Cambridge, Massachusetts. Pratt and Whitney bought the buildings and tore them down in 1963, removing the last vestiges of a company that thrived for more than half a century. (Roy Spiller collection.)

This photograph from the 1950s shows Interstate 84 (then Route 15) looking west from the area near the Forbes Street overpass. The large area of land then used for farming is presently devoted to commercial and industrial buildings. Present-day commuters can look with envy at the sparsely traveled highway that today is often the scene of bumper-to-bumper traffic. (Raymond Library collection.)

Recently picked tobacco is ready to be hung in a shed to dry. This photograph, taken in the early 20th century, is in the approximate location of the new Phillips Farm housing development near the corner of Forbes Street and Silver Lane. (Raymond Library collection.)

The Fred F. Leone and Sons' Silver Lane tobacco shed was typical of the many that dotted the landscape of East Hartford. Built in 1899, the barn was owned by Jim Harvey and was first located next to the present headquarters of Pratt and Whitney. In 1929, it was purchased for $300 and moved to Silver Lane by the Leone family. In 2008, the barn was moved again to another Leone family farm in Ellington. (Photograph by Buz Smucker.)

Mechanized vehicles were rapidly replacing horses in the harvesting of tobacco in the 1920s. This photograph shows some of the labor-intensive skills necessary to be a successful tobacco grower. Children were often let out of school to help harvest crops before hail or frost destroyed the plants. When East Hartford children were asked in school to draw a barn, they usually drew a tobacco shed, as that is what they were accustomed to seeing all over town. (Raymond Library collection.)

A good crop of broadleaf tobacco has just been picked and is hung on a horse-drawn wagon ready to be hung in a shed and cured. (Raymond Library collection.)

Tobacco growers in town found their business very profitable, and large plantations existed in all sections of East Hartford. Many people wanted to be part of this lucrative endeavor and bought shares of stock in the East Hartford Tobacco Growers, Inc. On December 12, 1923, R. J. Devitt purchased 10 shares at $100 per share, for a total of $1,000. This was no small amount, as the average yearly salary for Connecticut residents was $1,400. (Raymond Library collection.)

Rosina Annunziata Laraia (1896–1936) stands in the doorway of her home, once located at the northwest corner of Larrabee Street and Laraia Avenue. A tobacco shed stands on the left almost adjacent to the home. Daniel Laraia was born in the home and would raise his six children there. (Joan Laraia Martin collection.)

Rosina and John Laraia are shown here suckering broadleaf tobacco before harvesting in a field behind their home on Larrabee Street. Laraia Avenue now exists where these fields were, and the street was named in honor of John. (Joan Laraia Martin collection.)

This photograph shows farmers setting out their tobacco plants in the spring of 1902. Farmers still depended on horses for much of the hard labor, but the rapidly evolving automobile industry would soon provide equipment to ease their work and increase their crop yield. (Jessica Slade collection.)

Christian Handel is shown with his nine children in this c. 1850 photograph. From left to right are William, Pauline, Florence, Bethe, Mary, Albert, Ed, Rose, and Chris. The Handel family has been farming in town for more than a century. They still raise crops next to the Homestead Farm Dairy that they operate at 1441 Forbes Street. (Jessie Handel collection.)

Philip Handel III is shown with Ginger in this 1957 photograph taken at their Forbes Street farm. (Jessie Handel collection.)

On July 16, 1929, Faye Rentschler, wife of Frederick B. Rentschler, founder and president of Pratt and Whitney, broke ground for the new factory in East Hartford. Surrounding Faye are town and state officials. (United Technologies collection.)

This 1929 photograph shows the beginning stages of construction for the Pratt and Whitney aircraft engine plant. Sheds once used for drying tobacco now served as warehouses for heavy equipment. By 1930, the $2 million plant had a total area of 400,000 square feet and 30 test cells. (Pratt and Whitney Aircraft collection.)

Today Rentschler Field is home to the University of Connecticut football stadium and Cabela's first New England store. Soon the remaining acres will be developed into both business and residential areas. This May 1931 photograph shows numerous planes on the ground. Many notables in the aviation field such as Amelia Earhart, Charles Lindbergh, and Roscoe Turner were frequent visitors to Pratt and Whitney's Rentschler Field. The large areas of white in this photograph are shade-grown tobacco fields, clearly contrasting East Hartford's agricultural past with its booming manufacturing future. (United Technologies collection.)

Pratt and Whitney was founded by Frederick Rentschler in 1925 to manufacture air-cooled, radial aircraft engines. The company's first product was the Wasp, which initially powered navy and army air force fighters and some Boeing commercial planes. The company moved its headquarters to East Hartford in 1929. By this time, Pratt and Whitney's engines powered 90 percent of the nation's commercial aircraft and virtually all the navy's military aircraft. Over the years, Pratt and Whitney has maintained leadership in the aircraft engine industry, providing high-quality, dependable engines to power the country's premier military and commercial aircraft. (Ray Johnson collection.)

Original executives of Pratt and Whitney Aircraft are shown here with the 1,000th Wasp engine in 1928. Seen here are, from left to right, George J. Mead, vice president and engineering manager; Frederick B. Rentschler, president; Donald L. Brown, general manager; and William Willgoos, superintendent of assembly and test. (United Technologies collection.)

The hangar at Rentschler Field contained overhaul shops to service the famous Wasp and Hornet engines. The engines were disassembled, inspected, and reconditioned. In 1937, Rentschler Field was one of the busiest airports in New England and was the Connecticut terminal for American Airlines. Three flights daily provided passenger service to Boston and New York. (Raymond Johnson collection.)

Roscoe Turner, shown here at Rentschler Field, was one of the many aviation notables who visited Pratt and Whitney during the 1930s. He was born in 1895 at Corinth, Mississippi, and became a famous barnstormer in the 1920s. On November 14, 1930, he set the transcontinental airspeed record at 12 hours, 23 minutes from New York to California. He ran a flying school during World War II and trained 3,000 pilots. In 1952, he was awarded the Distinguished Flying Cross by the United States Congress. (United Technologies collection.)

44

During World War II, the companies that today comprise United Technologies employed thousands of people, a majority of them in East Hartford. Three shifts allowed the companies' machines to hum 24 hours a day. Huge traffic jams at shift changes were an everyday occurrence despite strict gas rationing. Workers who lived nearby were encouraged to walk, take a bus, or carpool to save gasoline needed for the war effort. As this vintage advertisement clearly shows, East Hartford was an important part of America's arsenal of democracy. (Francis Hoffman family collection.)

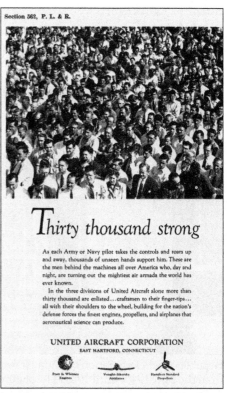

The advent of World War II brought thousands of people from throughout New England to East Hartford to work at Pratt and Whitney. The plant was running on three shifts, and suddenly a huge housing shortage existed in the area. Town residents rented out every available room but still could not meet the demand. One solution was the opening of trailer parks near Pratt and Whitney in an attempt to alleviate the problem. (Ray Johnson collection.)

Republic Steel Corporation's Union Drawn Steel Division operated a plant at 164 School Street from the early 1940s until 1983. The plant was originally built as a war plant during World War II to supply cold-finished steel bars and wire to New England's many machine shops producing the country's armaments. Peacetime operations primarily supplied bearing, hand tool, hardware, textile machine, and gun-manufacturing industries. LTV Steel Corporation purchased Republic Steel Corporation in 1983 and closed the plant in 1985. (Jack Sayre collection.)

Russell Turner is shown here operating a Lewis Wire straightening and cutting machine in the wire department of the Republic Steel Corporation. (Jack Sayre collection.)

East Hartford embraced the industrial age, as did the nation. The Hartford Clamp Company, presently located at 466 Park Avenue, was founded in 1917. The complexity of its work can be seen in this close-up of the pulleys that operated the machinery. (University of Connecticut, Thomas J. Dodd Research Center collection.)

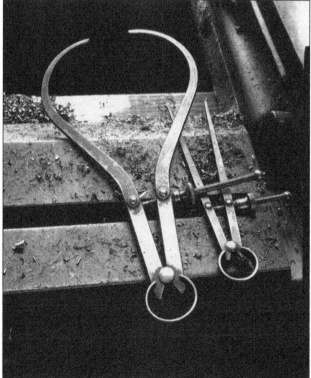

These calipers attest to the intricate work done by the Hartford Clamp Company. Today it continues to make clamps of all types, and its fine woodworker's clamps are still made on original machinery. The power for the machines comes from an extensive overhead line shaft system. (University of Connecticut, Thomas J. Dodd Research Center collection.)

Powerful pulleys helped operate precision machines such as this lathe at the Hartford Clamp Company. Metal shavings can be seen in the lower right-hand corner along with hand tools needed to create a finished product. (University of Connecticut, Thomas J. Dodd Research Center collection.)

In the 1950s and 1960s, East Hartford was known as the "Crossroads of New England." This aerial photograph of that era clearly shows how the moniker came about. Unfortunately, the construction of a new bridge and highways vastly disrupted neighborhoods located in the meadow section of town. (Raymond Library collection.)

Three

CONNECTICUT RIVER, THE GREAT DIVIDE

The Hartford Bridge, connecting the city to East Hartford, was the longest stone arch bridge in the world when it was built. It took three years to construct, and opening celebrations were held on October 6–8, 1908, with parades, fireworks, and historical pageants. Upon the death of Morgan G. Bulkeley in 1922, the bridge was named in his honor. Bulkeley had been mayor of Hartford, governor of Connecticut, and a state senator. (Richard Stevens family collection.)

The interior of the covered bridge between East Hartford and Hartford shows its sturdy construction. Trolley tracks ran through the middle of the bridge, and the first horse-drawn car crossed it in 1890. Tolls were charged for using the bridge. (University of Connecticut, Thomas J. Dodd Research Center collection.)

Burning of the Old Toll Bridge at Hartford, May 17, 1895.

On May 17, 1895, the covered wooden bridge known as "The Ark" caught fire and was totally destroyed. (Ray Johnson collection.)

Since East Hartford was first settled in the 1600s, crossing the Connecticut River to Hartford always presented a problem. During winter months, the frozen river could be crossed in wagons or on foot, but during other seasons the trip required a private boat, raft, or a ferry ride that cost money. The first bridge, a low wooden structure, was built in 1810, and a more substantial covered bridge was built in 1818. On the morning of May 18, 1895, this was all that remained of the old toll bridge that had been the only link between East Hartford and Hartford for 77 years. (Raymond Library collection.)

Ferryboat "F. C. Fowler," in use between Hartford and East Hartford after burning of Old Toll Bridge – 1895.

Once again people traveling between East Hartford and Hartford were forced to use ferries after the toll bridge burned. The ferryboat F. C. Fowler is ready to load passengers for their trip to East Hartford in 1895. (Ray Johnson collection.)

After the old toll bridge's destruction by fire, a temporary bridge was constructed as shown in this postcard. It opened for travel on June 12, 1896, and would remain in service until 1908 when the new Bulkeley Bridge would be dedicated. (Ray Johnson collection.)

The Hartford Bridge, later to be named the Bulkeley Bridge, opened in 1908. The first harness horse cart to cross the bridge that year was occupied by the Bennison children, properly dressed for the occasion. Queen B was the name of their pet horse, which provided the power for their ride. (Ray Johnson collection.)

52

On June 28, 1926, the Velodrome opened on the Connecticut River bank near the Bulkeley Bridge. The wooden structure cost $75,000 to build; 20,000 spectators could be seated inside. Professional boxing and football events were held there, and East Hartford High School's football team was allowed to play there. Primarily the Velodrome was built for professional bicycle racing, which was very popular in the 1920s. Teams from throughout the United States and Europe competed there. The structure was sold and dismantled in 1929. (Raymond Library collection.)

In the late 1920s and early 1930s, the *Kilarney* showboat, docked along the Connecticut River, was a popular restaurant and nightclub. It was owned by town resident O. Leo Quinn and other investors and was one of Greater Hartford's most popular attractions. The Great Depression was not kind to businesses, and this establishment fell victim to the woes of the nation's economy. (Ray Johnson collection.)

Silver Lane Grocery Store, located on the corner of Silver Lane and Main Street, suffered the ravages of the 1936 flood. The interior contents of the store were destroyed, creating an economic hardship for the Johnson family who owned the store. Likewise, area residents were deprived of needed supplies. (Robert Sukosky collection.)

A Connecticut Company bus skidded off the causeway on Main Street near Silver Lane during the 1936 flood. Over 500 town residents sought shelter in the high school as floodwaters reached a record-setting peak of 37.56 feet on March 21. The only means of communication for town residents was by way of shortwave radio, as 33 percent of East Hartford was covered with water. (Robert Sukosky collection.)

A news cameraman sits on an elevated platform near the corner of Main and Pitkin Streets recording the devastation brought to the town by the 1936 flood. (Robert Sukosky collection.)

On September 21, 1938, Connecticut and surrounding states were hammered by the winds of what would be known as the "Great New England Hurricane." With virtually none of the warning systems in place that exist today, damage was severe and widespread. This photograph shows School Street the morning after the storm. (Raymond Library collection.)

The 1936 flood ravaged much of the state of Connecticut and hit East Hartford especially hard due to its proximity to the Connecticut River. This photograph shows Main Street looking south toward Pitkin Street. (Raymond Library collection.)

The 1936 floodwaters nearly reached Main Street. Connecticut Boulevard is shown at the right, and Main Street is at the top of the picture. (Raymond Library collection.)

Members of the Burnham family examine damage to their Main Street neighborhood following the devastation of the 1938 hurricane. Today the Burnham family still farms the land, and their corn crops are eagerly awaited every year. Many local youths have earned their first wages picking corn before the sun rises to supply local markets and roadside stands. (Doris Haviland Timbrell collection.)

Damage was extensive throughout town from the Great New England Hurricane. This September 22, 1938, photograph shows Connecticut Company trolley No. 1565 stranded without power on Burnside Avenue. (Raymond Library collection.)

This 1938 photograph of Main Street near the South Windsor line shows the ravages left by the Great New England Hurricane. Residents relied on boats for transportation until the floodwaters subsided. (Doris Haviland Timbrell collection.)

Dutchland Farms, located at the corner of Pitkin and Main Streets, is surrounded by the floodwaters of 1936. The restaurant, on dry days, was known for its frankfurters, ice cream, and delicious coffee. The windmill on the top made the Dutchland Farms restaurants easily recognizable. (Robert Sukosky collection.)

Floodwaters ravaged the town in 1936 and again after the Great New England Hurricane of 1938. High-bodied cars of the 1930s, shown here, somehow managed to navigate the inundated streets. (Raymond Library collection.)

Gracious homes along upper Main Street were damaged in 1938, and tobacco crops were ruined. Today this area remains one of the last remnants of East Hartford's rich agricultural past, as the land is still extensively farmed. (Doris Haviland Timbrell collection.)

The Great New England Hurricane of September 21, 1938, struck East Hartford with a vengeance. Huge trees were ripped from the ground, as seen in this picture taken in front of Raymond Library on Main Street. Telephone and power lines were down for days, and floodwaters from the Connecticut River made travel by boat a necessity for many town residents. (Ray Johnson collection.)

Four

THE PUBLIC GOOD

Here is the East Hartford Police Department in 1931. Seen are, from left to right, (first row) Conrad Nutman, Max Knie, John Foley, William McKee, Timothy Kelleher, William Cooney, Frank O'Keefe, and Thomas Beakey; (second row) John Finley, John Fitzgerald, Ernest Hull, Ernest Amiot, Frank Norige, Daniel Collins, Frank Manor, Hugh Clancy, Lawrence Clancy, Hyram Caverley, Jack LaDuke, and Alfred Knie; (third row) officer Paniwitch, Leon Oshesky, William Kuebler, Frank Novello, Veto Bushnell, Michael McCarthy, Edward Tripp, Eugene Callahan, John Clancy, Michael Cavanaugh, Jerry Moynihan, George McClellan, and John Nagle. (G. William Miller collection.)

On October 17, 1974, Mayor Richard Blackstone (left) congratulates police officers who were recently promoted. Receiving their sergeant's badge are J. Brewster, James Keegan, and Otto Dowd. Looking on at right is police chief Clarence Drumm. (Raymond Library collection.)

In 1699, Daniel Bidwell was named constable for the portion of Hartford east of the river now known as East Hartford; however, the town would not get an official police department until 1895. John Bogue was sworn in as the town's first policeman on November 25, 1895. Today Chief Mark Sirois manages a well-equipped and well-trained police department, necessary for a town of almost 50,000 residents. This June 28, 1979, photograph shows the town's first annual police awards day ceremony. (Raymond Library collection.)

Elementary school students are on their way to Second North School on Main Street in this 1958 photograph. On Main Street, children shopped at the pet shop, a hobby shop next to Maxwell Drug Store, and a toy store near Woolworth's. Their parents could choose between three grocery stores, First National, Atlantic and Pacific, and Grand Union. If the family needed a new car, they could choose a new DeSoto at Eastwood Motors or visit the new rotunda-shaped showroom built by O'Meara Motors to sell the recently launched Edsel. (Raymond Library collection.)

This c. 1972 photograph was taken at a gathering of retired members of the East Hartford Police Department. Seen here are, from left to right, (first row) Lt. Lawrence Clancy, Assistant Chief John Gompper, Chief Timothy Kelleher, Chief Joseph Ciccalone, Lt. Otto Harry Miller, and Sgt. George Garrity; (second row) Sgt. John McGrath, officer John Davis, then chief Clarence Drumm, officer John Sullivan, officer Gibson Low, officer Raymond Kenyon, Lt. Peter Cipolla, and officer Sebastian Leone. (G. William Miller collection.)

Long before motorized apparatus was used, it was necessary to transport hose to a fire by hose reels. Note the large spoked wheels that carriages and buggies of the era possessed. Large hose reels were pulled by horse, but one this size would most likely be pulled by firemen. This hose reel from the beginning of the 20th century belonged to the Aetna Hose Company located on Connecticut Boulevard. (East Hartford Fire Department collection.)

Members of Center Hose Company No. 1 on Bissell Street proudly display their modern firefighting apparatus in this May 6, 1917, photograph. Sitting on the running board is Adolph Rosenthal; Al Carmel is standing on the rear of the truck under the number 1. (East Hartford Fire Department collection.)

Volunteer Hose Company No. 2 on Park Avenue was in use from 1893 until 1940, when a new and much larger firehouse was built farther north on Main Street. (East Hartford Fire Department collection.)

Aetna Hose Company, the fourth firehouse to be built in town, was constructed in 1893 on Connecticut Boulevard. Firefighting equipment was far different then, as the small hose cart indicates. All firefighters were volunteers, and when their service was needed, a large and very loud bell was rung in the center of town. The number of rings told firefighters where the fire was located. In 1903, the firehouse was abandoned and soon demolished for a right-of-way to the Bulkeley Bridge. (Raymond Library collection.)

In 1892, water mains were installed in town, facilitating the demise of bucket brigades to extinguish fires. Four firehouses were soon built throughout town. Volunteer Hose Company No. 2 was located near the corner of Main Street and Park Avenue. During the first half of the 20th century, volunteer firefighters competed in musters to show their skills. This Reo muster wagon belonged to Hose Company No. 2, and by the number of trophies displayed on the hood, it was indeed successful in its many competitions. (East Hartford Fire Department collection.)

Volunteer Hose Company No. 3 was located on Hanmer Street in the Burnside section of town. It was one of the original four firehouses built in town in the late 19th century once water mains and hydrants were installed. Members of the hose company shown here attest to the large number of town residents who volunteered their services. The building remains and is now used as a clubhouse. (East Hartford Fire Department collection.)

Fire alarm superintendent Henry Dawson inspects a Gamewell firebox as part of his job. Before the advent of the 911 telephone call, fires had to be reported by telephone or by pulling a lever on fireboxes located throughout town. Henry, a Beaumont Street resident, served in his position for many years. His wife Eleanor was the secretary at South Grammar School. (East Hartford Fire Department collection.)

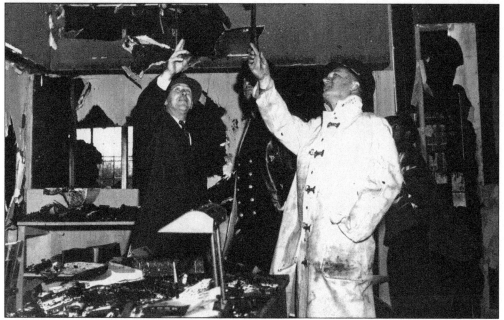

East Hartford fire chief Francis Dagon inspects the remains of the RCA building on Connecticut Boulevard. The November 12, 1957, fire was one of the town's most dangerous ones because the building housed numerous electrical components and supplies. (East Hartford Fire Department collection.)

The corner of Main and Brewer Streets is today home to Wendy's restaurant. Formerly it was home to the Brewer Shopping Center, which included a Popular Food Market plus many small stores that served the large number of people living in the southwestern portion of town. The whole complex was destroyed by fire in 1971. (East Hartford Fire Department collection.)

The interior of the Brewer Pharmacy was totally destroyed in 1971 when the Brewer Shopping Center caught fire. Firefighters are examining the debris for possible hot spots that could still be smoldering. In the white hat and coat is East Hartford Fire Department's Capt. Edward R. Johnson. (Ray Johnson collection.)

Smokey Bear greets Mayor John W. Torpey during Fire Prevention Week. Mayor Torpey, a Democrat, was first elected to the office in 1947 and would serve in that position for 16 years. His administration was known for its conservative fiscal policies and low tax rates that encouraged commercial, industrial, and residential growth. The 1956 Ford fire marshal's car indicates that this photograph was taken about that time. (Raymond Library collection.)

Stanley and Nap, a popular electronics store and service center, was destroyed by fire on March 7, 1958. The building was located at the rear of 385 Main Street. (East Hartford Fire Department collection.)

A town parade in the 1950s proudly showcases the apparatus of the East Hartford Fire Department along with the chief's shiny 1955 Pontiac. (East Hartford Fire Department collection.)

Firefighters and police officers often spend weekends and holidays away from their families. This 1950s photograph shows firefighters at headquarters on Main Street preparing to celebrate Thanksgiving, hoping a fire call will not interrupt their meal. (East Hartford Fire Department collection.)

The Hollister family lived in this beautiful Victorian home at 320 Silver Lane, a bit east of the present-day Taco Bell restaurant. (Ray Johnson collection.)

In the 1970s, the Hollister home caught fire and was completely destroyed. (East Hartford Fire Department collection.)

The Hockanum Hose Company Museum is located behind East Hartford Fire Station No. 6 at 1050 Forbes Street. The museum contains fire apparatus, memorabilia, and photographs related to the fire department's history. Highlighting the numerous exhibits is a 1940 Mack 600-gallon-per-minute pumper in its original condition. When the fire department retired the 1940 Mack truck, affectionately known as "Maxine," local firefighters spearheaded a drive to save the truck. A building on Silver Lane was donated, and firefighters moved it to Forbes Street. While many helped with the museum, the majority of the work was done by Robert Barno, Myles Byrnes, and George Crowley. (East of the River Tourism District collection.)

Today people throng to stores to buy the newest iPhone or BlackBerry or form lines to see the latest movie. The concept is not new, as this photograph reveals. Trolley service from East Hartford to Glastonbury was inaugurated in 1892, and it is doubtful that all these prospective passengers got to have a ride. (University of Connecticut, Thomas J. Dodd Research Center collection.)

This 1910 picture of Main Street shows several buildings that still grace downtown. The differences, however, are very apparent. No automobiles are visible, as the trolley was the main means of transportation for most town residents. The milk wagon and another horse-drawn wagon illustrate the way goods were delivered at the beginning of the 20th century. (Roy Spiller collection.)

An interurban trolley stands at the intersection of Connecticut Boulevard (then Hartford Avenue). In the early 1900s, interurban cars would travel on trolley tracks but would then transfer to railroad tracks to service towns far away where regular trolley service did not exist. (Roy Spiller collection.)

This Connecticut Company (Hartford Division) trolley was photographed on August 5, 1934, at station No. 24 near the present-day Hockanum School. Trolley stops were designated by numbers, and residents would often indicate to others where they lived by the closest station number. The bright yellow trolleys were a familiar sight to citizens and provided an excellent mass transit system. (University of Connecticut, Thomas J. Dodd Research Center collection.)

People driving down Main Street today would be startled to come across a trolley pulling freight cars; however, this sight was a matter-of-fact occurrence for many years, as shown in this August 31, 1934, photograph of Connecticut Company trolley No. 2023 at Hockanum station No. 20. (Photograph by Roger Borrup.)

This freight trolley makes a right turn from Burnside Avenue onto Church Street to deliver a load of coal to the Taylor-Atkins mill. The mill made writing paper, tablets, papeteries, envelopes, and stationery supplies. The year was 1937, and the motorman could stop at the First National store in Burnside center on his return trip, where butter was 41¢ per pound, pork chops cost 39¢ a pound, and a Baby Ruth candy bar cost 5¢. (Ray Johnson collection.)

The Connecticut Company trolley barn was located on Main Street where the town hall is today. Built in 1892 by the East Hartford and Glastonbury Horse Railroad Company, it was razed in the 1930s. Trolleys were stored there for routes east of the Connecticut River. (Robert Sukosky collection.)

This four-car freight trolley rumbles down Main Street in front of the Raymond Library on a winter day in 1930. A year earlier similar freight trolleys moved all of Pratt and Whitney's machines and equipment from Hartford to the new East Hartford plant in four days. (Roy Spiller collection.)

In 1935, freight trains regularly traveled down Main Street. This photograph shows one approaching Burnside Avenue having just left the freight yard. It is headed for Glastonbury. (Raymond Library collection.)

St. John's Episcopal Church on Main Street is in the background as Connecticut Company trolley No. 1303 travels from the Woodland section of town to Hartford. When this photograph was taken in 1934, East Hartford and the nation were in the throes of the Great Depression. On Connecticut Boulevard, also known then and now as "Automobile Row," a new Ford could be purchased for $585 by the few who could afford one. (Ray Johnson collection.)

The land for the Raymond Library was given to the town in 1879 by Albert C. Raymond, a farmer and businessman. Upon his death in 1880, he willed money to the town for the construction of a library. The Raymond Library was built between 1888 and 1889 at a cost of $6,500. Its dedication was a major event, attended by most of the town's residents. With its elegant Romanesque Revival library, East Hartford was beginning to change its totally rural appearance to one of a prosperous town, although agriculture remained its primary industry. (Roy Spiller collection.)

Very few small communities have a bus company named after one of their main thoroughfares. The Silver Lane Bus Company's buses ran the length of Silver Lane on their route from Manchester to Hartford. Noted for its friendly drivers, the bus company is still fondly remembered today. After World War II, East Hartford experienced a massive home-building boom, primarily in the farmlands of the south end. Many of the town's new residents daily rode the red and green buses to their jobs in Hartford. (Manchester Historical Society.)

CHARTER SERVICE

Buses for Hire for
SPECIAL PARTIES
at Reasonable Rates

Hartford **THE SHORTEST LINE** Manchester
Shopping ◄──── Between ────► Shopping
Center **THESE TWO POINTS** Center

THE SILVER LANE BUS LINE

GENERAL INFORMATION

Children five (5) years of age or over, full fare.

Holiday Schedule will be operated on New Years Day, Memorial Day, Independence Day, Labor Day, Thanksgiving Day, Christmas Day.

We will at all times give full consideration to suggestions for improvements in the service. Stops in Manchester, East Hartford, and Hartford on our lines will coincide with the revised stops of the other transportation companies.

- Manchester Shopping District
- Cheney Brothers
- Pioneer Parachute Company
- Independent Cloak Company
- Cooper Hill Apartments
- Orford Village
- Manchester Housing Authority
- Silver Lane
- Pratt & Whitney
- East Hartford
- Hartford Shopping Center

OWNED AND OPERATED BY
SILVER LANE BUS LINE, INCORPORATED
49 Brainard Place
Manchester, Connecticut

TELEPHONES

Days: MItchell 3-8978
Nights: MItchell 9-9735

Effective, Sunday, May 7, 1961
EASTERN STANDARD TIME

During the period Daylight Saving is in effect read as
DAYLIGHT SAVING TIME

Subject to Change without notice
Not responsible for delays

Approved by the
Connecticut Public Utilities Commission

This Silver Lane Bus Line schedule dates from the 1950s and lists the excellent service the company provided. (Roy Spiller collection.)

Veterans Memorial Clubhouse, located at 100 Sunset Ridge Drive, opened in 1930 as the clubhouse for the Sunset Ridge Golf Club, a private nine-hole course. Located on the second-highest spot in town, it was taken over by the U.S. Army in 1942, and anti-aircraft batteries were installed on the grounds to protect Pratt and Whitney during World War II. In 1949, Pratt and Whitney purchased the building and surrounding 50 acres of land and donated it to the town in memory of workers who lost their lives in World War II. (Roy Spiller collection.)

East Hartford had its own hospital in the early 1950s, as shown in this photograph. Located on Main Street across from town hall, the structure shown here is now one wing of the Riverside Health Care Center. (Burton H. Anderson collection.)

Donald Hallquist was a much-admired music teacher and assistant superintendent in the East Hartford school system. Upon his early retirement, he worked for the First Federal Savings Bank. After retiring from the bank, he was active with the East Hartford Chamber of Commerce, the School Business Partnership, and the Rotary Club while serving as organist and music director at South Congregational Church. He died in February 2007. (Donald Hallquist Jr. collection.)

On June 3, 1953, a large crowd attended the cornerstone laying of the new East Hartford High School, which was built on approximately 30 acres of the former Goodwin property on Burnside Avenue. The ultramodern structure replaced the former high school on Chapman Street and was the envy of surrounding towns. Today it is used as the East Hartford Middle School and houses seventh- and eighth-grade students from the whole town. (Raymond Library collection.)

Meadow Hill, one of the town's senior housing complexes, provides comfortable living standards, friendship, and many opportunities to socialize, as this 1966 photograph indicates. (Raymond Library collection.)

Miss Williams poses with her class of 30 students in this 1885 photograph. Many familiar family names in town are among the students, including Carroll, Bidwell, Garrity, and Olmsted. (Raymond Library collection.)

This billboard was erected in the early 1950s for a twofold purpose. New homes were sprouting up all over town to house parents and their baby boomer children, who were being born in record numbers. The sign alerted drivers to be careful of these children and also sent a message that East Hartford was a great place to live. (Ray Johnson collection.)

By the late 1930s, passenger trolley service would be gone from town, and from that point on the bus would reign supreme. The removal of tracks created traffic havoc, but the scrap metal would contribute to the rapidly growing defense industries in the country. (University of Connecticut, Thomas J. Dodd Research Center collection.)

New telephone cable arrives at the corner of Connecticut Boulevard and Prospect Street. (Southern New England Telephone Company Records, Archives and Special Collections at the Thomas J. Dodd Research Center, University of Connecticut Libraries.)

After the 1936 flood, new telephone cable had to be installed throughout the sections of town that had been under water. (Southern New England Telephone Company Records, Archives and Special Collections at the Thomas J. Dodd Research Center, University of Connecticut Libraries.)

Young baby boomers board a bus for a ride home after a busy day at Burnside School in 1958. Elementary school enrollment in town that year was just shy of 7,000 students, with 503 being housed at Burnside School. School overcrowding was still a problem because of the town's rapidly growing population, forcing the town to still use the wooden structure in Mayberry Village affectionately known as "Little Red Schoolhouse," with additional students being taught at the Mayberry Community Building. (Raymond Library collection.)

Five

GOOD TIMES SHARED

Main Street 1946

Since its beginning, Augie and Ray's has been a favorite stop for a special meal. It is hard to find anyone in central Connecticut who has not been to the restaurant, and it is known far and wide for its delicious food and superb service. It is still owned and operated by members of the Hutt family. (Ernie Hutt collection.)

Ray Hutt and Augie Bria, two former East Hartford policemen, decided in 1946 to open Augie and Ray's Milk Bar. They figured the location adjacent to Pratt and Whitney on Main Street would be lucrative, and 63 years later, the restaurant is still serving some of the tastiest food in the area. (Ernie Hutt collection.)

By 1958, Augie and Ray's had outgrown the original location. Their new, much larger restaurant can be seen in the background. The original building would be demolished, and the new facility would carry the tradition of delicious food, including Ray Hutt's original recipe for chili sauce and their famous onion rings. (Ernie Hutt collection.)

The Marco Polo Restaurant on Burnside Avenue is still one of East Hartford's favorite restaurants. This early-1950s postcard lists the "Blue Plate Specials," which included veal scaloppini, chicken cacciatore, lobster, and scallops. All meals came with spaghetti, garden salad, and fries. The back of the card states that "Kilroy was here and he had a wonderful time." (Ray Johnson collection.)

The Puritan Maid Restaurant on Connecticut Boulevard was a familiar town landmark for many years along with being a favorite stop for good food. It was owned and operated by the Wooldridge Brothers, and restaurants of the same design were located in Hartford, Farmington, Wethersfield, and Avon. In the 1950s, the building was converted into the Dworin Chevrolet dealership. Eventually the building was torn down, and the site is now home to the Gengras Chrysler, Dodge, and Jeep dealership. (Ray Johnson collection.)

The Triangle Snack Bar, located at 171 Governor Street, was one of many mom-and-pop establishments throughout town in the 1950s. When this photograph was taken in 1953, the Stop and Shop on Burnside Avenue featured eggs for 74¢ a dozen and a Betty Crocker cake mix cost 35¢. A first-class stamp was 3¢ at the post office on Main Street. (Roy Spiller collection.)

Once known as the Brewer Block, Church Corners Inn today appears much as it did in this 1930s postcard. Located on Main Street across from Connecticut Boulevard, it has served as a hotel and restaurant for many decades. (Raymond Library collection.)

O'Brien's Diner was located at 668 Connecticut Boulevard and was known for its delicious breakfast platters. When this picture was taken in 1956, the average price of a new home in East Hartford was $16,000, a man's topcoat at Sage-Allen on Main Street cost $59.98, and a roll of camera film was 45¢ at People's Drug Store on Burnside Avenue. (Roy Spiller collection.)

Sage-Allen, East Hartford's largest department store, was three years old in 1943 when this advertisement appeared. Shoes were rationed in February, but one could still purchase an Arrow dress shirt for $2.75 or a lady's Benrus 15-jewel watch for $24.75. Town residents did their grocery shopping at several small stores throughout town. Those included Manierre's and Nemerow's on Burnside Avenue, Levine's on Ward Street, and Hoffman's on Church Street. Canned goods, coffee, and sugar were rationed, but one could purchase a beef rib roast for 35¢ per pound or dried prunes for 14¢ per pound. (Francis Hoffman family collection.)

Liberty Stores, East Hartford, Conn.

This picture of Main Street during the late 1940s or early 1950s shows several of the local businesses. At this time, residents took care of their shopping needs at Sage-Allen Department Store, Landau's Department Store, Harmac's Men's Shop, Maxwell Drug Store, F. W. Woolworth's, and many other shops. Friday nights saw stores staying open later, and throngs of shoppers eagerly spent their week's wages. (Ray Johnson collection.)

Throughout the United States, the 1950s was a time that witnessed a new concept in commercial construction—the shopping center. In 1958, East Hartford joined the ranks of other towns across the country with a new shopping center on Silver Lane anchored by the J. M. Fields discount store. While these new shopping centers were eagerly embraced by consumers, few at the time realized that they would be responsible for the gradual decline of downtowns everywhere. (Raymond Library collection.)

During the holidays, or at any time of the year, the Candy Box store located at the Burnham and Brady Candy Company on Burnside Avenue was a great place to visit. Christmas and Easter found long lines waiting to enter the store that, without question, had the best aroma in town. Their chocolate-dipped strawberries were eagerly awaited each June and were sold at their store and at G. Fox and Company in downtown Hartford. The company began its business in 1925 in the building shown here, which once was a tobacco warehouse. (Ray Johnson collection.)

The Hockanum Post Office was located at what is now 224 Main Street. In the early 1900s, it housed the Harold E. Brewer Ice Cream Parlor as well as the post office. Brewer's mother served as postmistress. Needless to say, it was a favorite spot of local children. Farmhands who labored for long hours in the nearby tobacco fields would frequently stop for a treat of homemade ice cream. (Raymond Library collection.)

Anderson Jewelers, a venerable town landmark, has been located at 1015 Main Street since 1929. Herb Anderson, shown in this 1930s photograph, purchased the jewelry store in November 1929. Anderson, who resided on Harrison Place, ran the business until 1968, when he turned it over to the present owner, George Agnelli Sr., later joined by his son, George Agnelli Jr. A wide selection of quality items and outstanding service has allowed this East Hartford store to remain in business for 80 years. (Agnelli family collection.)

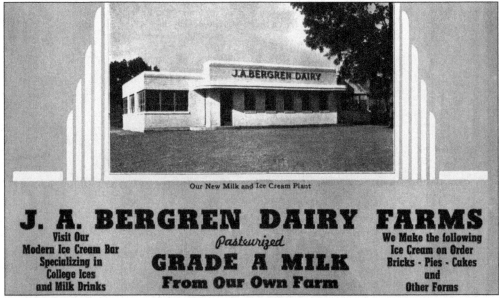

Our New Milk and Ice Cream Plant

J. A. BERGREN DAIRY FARMS

Visit Our
Modern Ice Cream Bar
Specializing in
College Ices
and Milk Drinks

Pasteurized

GRADE A MILK

From Our Own Farm

We Make the following
Ice Cream on Order
Bricks - Pies - Cakes
and
Other Forms

By 1940, Bergren's Dairy had built its new ice-cream bar/restaurant building shown in this picture. The milk from Bergren's own cows was used for grade A milk only. Milk bought from neighboring Wickham farm and Cannon farm, as well as from farms in Ellington, was used for other dairy products. In the late 1960s, Arthur Bergren sold the business to Knudsen Farms. (Roy Spiller collection.)

The Bergren home on Burnside Avenue is shown in this photograph taken about 1930. Deliveryman Bill Knie is about to begin his daily rounds. (G. William Miller collection.)

By the time Bergren's Dairy replaced its horse-drawn delivery wagons with motorized trucks, it had built its residential delivery business up to 40 routes. Two wholesale trucks delivered bottled milk to grocery stores and restaurants. Interestingly, the company's best driver was given the first motorized truck for his delivery route. After two weeks and three accidents, that driver quit to go to work at a dairy that still used horses. (Betty Bergren Martocchio collection.)

Brothers John and Albert Bergren emigrated from Sweden in 1906 to work at the Cheney Mill in Manchester. In approximately 1910, they founded their fledgling dairy business. Albert stayed active in the business for only a few years, leaving John and his wife, Julia, as owner/operators. Starting out with only a few cows and a horse-and-buggy delivery van, they eventually grew the business through the late 1920s when their son Arthur became active in the day-to-day operation. (Betty Bergren Martocchio collection.)

The back of the Bergren Dairy Company at 1100 Burnside Avenue is shown here at the time when both horse-drawn and motorized vehicles were used. Shown here are, from left to right, five horse-drawn wagons, three trucks, and a large Mack truck used to pick up cans of milk from farms. (Betty Bergren Martocchio collection.)

This 1930s photograph shows a family reunion at the saltbox home of Benjamin and Katherine Prasser on Forbes Street. Ben Prasser was a farmer (note the corncrib to the left of the photograph) and also serviced and installed well pumps. Today a residential street in town is named after the Prasser family. (Doris Haviland Timbrell collection.)

The Benjamin Prasser home, built around 1790, is also known as the Samuel Arnold Jr. home. The original owner of the home was Ashbel Roberts, who sold the house to Arnold in 1795. When the home faced demolition due to the construction of new homes on Heritage Drive, the East Hartford Historical Society rallied for its preservation. It was moved several feet south, and restoration work was done by the Greater Hartford Architectural Conservancy. Today privately owned, the red farmhouse sits adjacent to fields of corn on Forbes Street near the corner of Heritage Drive. (Photograph by Bill Secord.)

Raymond C. "Joe" Dunn was a true Renaissance man and a man for all seasons, but Christmas was special to him. Joe started creating Christmas displays at his home at 166 Silver Lane in 1936 and continued for about 10 years. His displays were so popular that people traveled from every corner of the state to see them. Joe led a very interesting life. He started his working career as a car salesman. He then worked for Socony Oil before moving on to Pratt and Whitney in 1940 to help with the war effort. After he retired, he worked for G. Fox and Company during Christmas as Santa Claus, the job he liked the most. (Roy Spiller collection.)

One of the many Christmas displays erected by Raymond C. Dunn at his Silver Lane home included the beautiful Victorian-era coach surrounded by life-sized carolers clad in outfits typical of that time period. (Roy Spiller collection.)

The William Smith house, located at 166 Silver Lane, is one of the town's last remaining 18th-century, one-and-a-half-story farmhouses. The home was built a year before the dirt path in front of it became town property, necessitating William Smith to work out an agreement with neighbor Benjamin Hills for permission to use the road to reach his home. This photograph shows the home in the 1930s or 1940s when it was owned by Raymond C. Dunn, who was noted for his spectacular Christmas displays. (Roy Spiller collection.)

This picture shows another one of Dunn's many outstanding Christmas displays. People from far and wide traveled to see Dunn's displays each year, and major traffic jams occurred, requiring a police officer to keep the traffic flowing. A contest was held each year in Hartford County with awards given to the most outstanding Christmas display at a private residence. The contest was finally discontinued, as Dunn won the prize every year, undoubtedly discouraging others in surrounding towns to enter. (Roy Spiller collection.)

Theresa Lombardi, age 11, a student at the Hockanum Elementary School, participated in the 1973 Halloween window-painting contest sponsored by the East Hartford Chamber of Commerce. She is decorating the window of Arthur's Fine Foods on Main Street, currently the site of the Save-A-Lot Supermarket. Store windows throughout town were decorated with festive Halloween scenes painted by students from every school. (Raymond Library collection.)

Arthur H. and Amie W. Gaines, the parents of Jessie Slade, take a pleasant buggy ride along Silver Lane, as shown in this 1903 photograph. They traveled on a narrow dirt roadway, and their view would mainly have consisted of farmland. (Jessica Slade collection.)

Members of the East Hartford Bicentennial Commission await the arrival of the French troop reenactors at the East Hartford–Manchester town line on Silver Lane. The two-year bicentennial celebration lasted from 1975 to 1976, both nationally and town wide. Standing left of the sign are Mayor Richard Blackstone and his wife, Terrye. Terrye did a highly commendable job as chairperson of the East Hartford Bicentennial Commission. (Raymond Library collection.)

The year 1976 again saw French troops marching down Silver Lane as they had done in 1781. This time, however, they were American reenactors commemorating Comte de Rochambeau's march from Newport, Rhode Island, to New York to join forces with Gen. George Washington's army. The march was one of the many events celebrated nationally for the American Revolution Bicentennial. Three East Hartford residents completed the full march; they are, from left to right, Tom Sayer, Anthony Fornabi, and Tom Fornabi. (Raymond Library collection.).

Reenactors of Comte de Rochambeau's march launch their boat across the Connecticut River in the same manner as Count Jean Baptiste de Rochambeau and his 5,000 French troops in 1781 after their encampment on Silver Lane. (Raymond Library collection.)

In 1976, the American Revolution Bicentennial flag was presented to the town, and it would fly in front of town hall for the whole year. Standing here are, from left to right, Hazel Ireland, United States national bicentennial representative; George Cyr, Connecticut bicentennial chairman; Mayor Richard Blackstone; and Terrye Blackstone, East Hartford bicentennial chairperson. (Raymond Library collection.)

As part of the town's celebration of the American Revolution Bicentennial, two Elizabethan dinners were held in 1975 and 1976. The University of Connecticut Madrigal Singers shown here performed at the 1975 dinner. South Congregational Church on Forbes Street hosted the event, and tickets were very hard to get due to its popularity. (Raymond Library collection.)

Art Buchwald (1925–2007) was one of the many notables to visit town during the 1970s. He was an American humorist best known for his *Washington Post* political satire column that was syndicated in newspapers throughout the world. The Pulitzer Prize winner is shown here with Mayor Richard Blackstone and his wife, Terrye. His evening appearance at East Hartford High School played to a standing-room-only audience. (Terrye Blackstone collection.)

This plaque, located in front of town hall, gives a brief history of East Hartford. Every town in Connecticut received one during the 1975–1976 celebration of the American Revolution Bicentennial. (Raymond Library collection.)

In 1983, East Hartford celebrated its 200th anniversary as a town, having successfully separated from Hartford in 1783. Many activities took place throughout the year, including the crowning of a queen. East Hartford's bicentennial queen was Margaret B. Spiller (center) with her court Jean L. DellaRocca (left) and Janet Harlow (right). (Roy Spiller collection.)

LE BAL TABARIN

MOST BEAUTIFUL DANCE PALACE IN AMERICA

HARTFORD, CONN. JUST OVER THE BRIDGE.

While this postcard gives the address of Le Bal Tabarin as Hartford, it was actually in East Hartford on Connecticut Boulevard just east of the Bulkeley Bridge. It was built in 1915 as a skating rink and, in 1920, converted to an upscale dining and dancing establishment at a cost of $75,000. This was a huge amount of money when a new home could be purchased in town for under $5,000, and the average yearly salary of local residents was approximately $1,500. (Roy Spiller collection.)

Big name bands played at Le Bal Tabarin during the Roaring Twenties, as shown in this photograph. Balconies were located on both sides of the ballroom, allowing diners to view the dancers below. Extravagantly decorated and serving delicious food, Le Bal Tabarin attracted visitors from throughout the state. A massive fire in 1926 destroyed the building. Shortly after the fire, the land would be used to construct the Velodrome. (Roy Spiller collection.)

Rev. William Flynn of the First Congregational Church and Jessie Slade are ready to participate in one of the many events that took place in 1983 to celebrate East Hartford's bicentennial. Jessie is fondly remembered as the "Trunk Lady" by hundreds of the town's students. Under the auspices of the East Hartford Historical Society, Jessie visited all elementary schools in town accompanied by an antique trunk filled with items from the past. Children were in awe of candlesnuffers, soap savers, and a variety of other items no longer commonly seen. (Jessica Slade collection.)

Six
COMING TOGETHER

East Hartford High School was founded in 1883, and classes began in 1886 at the building that later served as Center School on Main Street at Church Corners. At the time, a high school education was completed in three years. The building seen here, a wooden structure with a slate roof, was constructed in 1895 at the corner of Chapman and Main Streets. Before 1883, town students seeking a high school education had to apply for acceptance at Hartford Public High School. The building would serve the town for only 20 years, as it burned down in 1915. (Roy Spiller collection.)

The Goodwin one-room schoolhouse is presently situated in Martin Park. Originally it was located behind the Goodwin homestead on Burnside Avenue, adjacent to East Hartford Middle School. This 1975 photograph shows it being moved to its current site. The school was a gift to the town from George Goodwin, grandson of the original builder, who constructed it in 1821 to educate his eight children. (Raymond Library collection.)

This beautiful building was erected on Main Street in 1832 to house the East Hartford Select School, later renamed the Classical and English School. It was a private academy that attracted students from throughout the United States and from foreign countries. By 1883, the building was owned by Jonathan Wells, who gave it to the town in that year. It became East Hartford's first town hall. It is fitting that this building has recently been restored to its original grandeur and now houses the East Hartford Board of Education. (Roy Spiller collection.)

For many decades, the Town Hall Inn, located at 1110 Main Street, was a favorite dining spot. While this photograph dates from the 1970s, an April 29, 1945, menu tells much about a different era. A whole live broiled lobster was listed at $2, grilled pork chops cost $1.55, while broiled sweetbreads and mushrooms would set the customer back $1.65. All meals came with an appetizer, vegetables, dessert, and beverage. Noted on the back of the menu was a message apologizing to customers for certain food shortages due to wartime conditions. (Raymond Library collection.)

It is appropriate that this beautiful building located at 1110 Main Street is today home to the East Hartford Board of Education. Built in 1832 as the East Hartford Select School, a private academy, it was later known as the Classical and English School. The building also once served as East Hartford's town hall. (Photograph by Bill Secord.)

Center School, located on Main Street across from Connecticut Boulevard (then Hartford Avenue), was built in 1856. It was one of the best-equipped schools in East Hartford, with the town picking up most of the cost of supplies. Despite this support, teacher turnover was a major problem due to extremely low salaries. Much like today, parents were encouraged to play a major role in their children's education. The student population would always decrease in late spring, as children were needed to help their parents prepare gardens and plant crops. (Roy Spiller collection.)

The original Hockanum School, located at 165 Main Street, was built around 1870 on land purchased from William Jones. By the 1940s, the two-room school was on double session, and four kindergartens were housed in portable classrooms. Because of the tremendous population growth in the south end of town, a new, much larger Hockanum School opened in 1949 nearby at 191 Main Street. For many years, the old school served as the Hockanum Library, a branch of the Raymond Library. (Robert Sukosky collection.)

This 1908 photograph shows a one-room schoolhouse that was located on Main Street just south of Silver Lane. Class sizes were about what they are today, but students of varying ages would share the same classroom. Based on the teacher's expression, it is doubtful that discipline was a problem. (Ray Johnson collection.)

This one-room schoolhouse was located on Long Hill Street. The teacher received free board with families of students and would stay longer at the homes of large families since they had more children in school. Books and supplies were not provided by the town and had to be purchased by the students' families. Individual slates were used for writing practice along with papers sewn together to form notepads. (Roy Spiller collection.)

Union School, a two-story wooden structure, was located on the north side of Burnside Avenue across from present-day Ecology Drive. Miss Geraldine Butters, a favorite fifth-grade teacher, yearly held an eagerly anticipated spelling bee with girls competing against the boys. The winning team would receive special treats at Miss Butters's home. As was the custom of the day, girls entered the building through one door while boys entered through a different one. (Roy Spiller collection.)

East Hartford High School on Chapman Street opened in 1917, and its first graduating class in 1918 is pictured here. After fire destroyed the wooden high school on Main Street, students were housed in various buildings throughout town until this brick edifice was constructed. Students who did not live within walking distance of the high school were given a discount rate on the town trolleys. Today the building serves as the East Hartford Cultural Center. (Raymond Library collection.)

East Hartford High School's football team is shown in this 1920 photograph taken in front of the new school on Chapman Street. In this year, the town's population was just shy of 12,000 and was growing at a faster rate than neighboring Hartford. (Roy Spiller collection.)

The year was 1920, and Woodrow Wilson was president. The Red Sox traded Babe Ruth to the Yankees, and Prohibition had been in effect since January 16. The United States population was 106 million, and 11,648 people called East Hartford home. Shown here is the East Hartford High School baseball team for the 1920 season. Most homes in town had a radio, and the music of choice for young people was jazz. According to an advertisement in the *Hartford Courant*, a person could buy a new seven-room house on Burnside Avenue for $4,300. (Roy Spiller collection.)

The Center Grammar School was located on Main Street at the intersection of Connecticut Boulevard next to the present-day Church Corners Inn. This photograph shows the 1929 graduating class. (Richard Stevens family.)

This 1941 photograph shows the First North School, located on the north side of Gilman Street. The 1,144-square-foot, one-story frame building had an insurance value of $6,669 in 1941. (Robert Sukosky collection.)

Town pride translated to intense school spirit at East Hartford High School. By the early 1950s, the high school was fielding varsity teams in football, baseball, cross-country, track, wrestling, and tennis. Pictured above are the 1952 East Hartford Hornets' cheerleaders, the only varsity sport open to girls at that time. They are, from left to right, (first row) Sue Colmer, little Carolyn Kurth, Ellen Welsh, Margie Imeln, Joan Ellis, Roberta Adams, Lorraine Griffith, and Elaine Davy; (second row) Carol Holmes, Jackie Tully, Nedra Ulm, and Frank Hatchett. (Jackie Danise collection.)

This brownstone monument in Center Cemetery honors those from town who served in the Civil War. The population of East Hartford at the start of the war was about 3,000, and nearly 300 residents served in the Union army. Approximately 30 town residents died in the conflict, including a free black soldier named Samuel Francis. Two East Hartford soldiers died at the notorious Andersonville Prison. (Photograph by Bill Secord.)

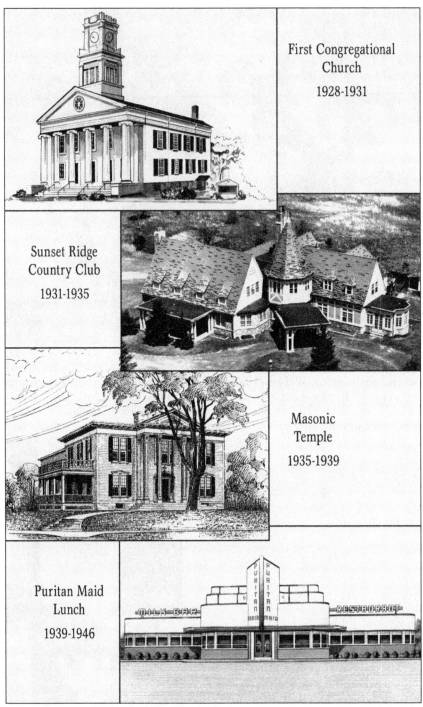

First Congregational Church
1928-1931

Sunset Ridge Country Club
1931-1935

Masonic Temple
1935-1939

Puritan Maid Lunch
1939-1946

Since 1928 the East Hartford Rotary Club has held its weekly meeting at eight different locations. Meetings initially began in 1928 at the First Congregational Church on Main Street and then moved to the newly opened Sunset Ridge Country Club. From there, meetings continued at the Masonic temple on Main Street and the Puritan Maid Restaurant on Connecticut Boulevard. (Roy Spiller collection.)

114

Town Hall Inn
and Diner
1946-1947

Old Colony
Restaurant
1947-1960

Church Corners
Inn
1960-1967

Veterans Memorial
Club House
1967-present

The Town Hall Inn and Diner on Main Street hosted Rotary Club meetings next before a move to the Old Colony Restaurant, which was located on the Connecticut Boulevard just east of the Bulkeley Bridge. Church Corners Inn on Main Street served as the next meeting location before a move to the current site. Meetings now occur every Wednesday at the Veteran's Memorial Clubhouse on Sunset Ridge Drive in the building that once was home to the Sunset Ridge Country Club. (Roy Spiller collection.)

Early in the 20th century, children skated on Long Pond under the Connecticut Boulevard (then Hartford Avenue) causeway. Today the water is no more, and where the skaters are is now the Governor Street exit of Interstate 84. (Roy Spiller collection.)

During World War II and for many years after, this roll of honor was displayed in town and listed all East Hartford residents who had served in the military. During the 1950s, it was placed in front of Woodland School, where students proudly found the names of their parents. (Ray Johnson collection.)

East Hartford citizens dedicated its World War I monument, located in front of Raymond Library, on October 5, 1929. It is a life-size bronze rendering of a World War I infantryman, fondly known as a doughboy. Citizens of the town raised $7,000 for the statue, which was the work of William Allenwood Murphy of Hartford. (Photograph by Bill Secord.)

The Rotary Eternal Light for Peace sits proudly in front of the Raymond Library on Main Street. A similar one exists in Neath, Glam, Wales, in the United Kingdom. The two torches were dedicated on April 18, 1965, and both were lit simultaneously through a telephone connection via Tel Star satellite. (Photograph by Bill Secord.)

Shortly after Pratt and Whitney gave the former Sunset Ridge Country Club (now known as Veteran's Memorial Clubhouse) to the town in 1949, a soapbox derby track was built on an adjacent steep slope, parallel to Route 15. Young people, at first only boys, from throughout the state competed here with the winner going to the finals in Akron, Ohio. James Dinsmore was the first local boy to win the state championship. (East Hartford Fire Department collection.)

Martin Park has been at its Burnside Avenue location since 1921 on land formerly owned by the Gibbons family. The 24-acre park has baseball fields, a wading pool, a swimming pool, and tennis courts built in 1935 by the Works Progress Administration. Martin Park is named after a beloved local priest, Fr. J. Clement Martin, who was an avid sports fan. For many years, Martin Park was the location where East Hartford held its huge fireworks display every July 4. (Raymond Library collection.)

On November 10, 1969, town clerk Wilma Older swears in newly elected town leaders. In that year, schools were bursting at their seams with 9,269 students enrolled in elementary schools; 1,703 at East Hartford High School; and 1,873 at Penney High School. New teachers were hired at a salary of $6,300 per year. (Raymond Library collection.)

In the mid-1970s the federal hourly minimum wage was $2.10, regular gasoline sold for 60¢ a gallon, and the place to be for town youngsters was in the East Hartford Midget Football Program. More than 300 children participated in the four teams—the Cardinals, coached by Ray Micoletti; the Elks, coached by Bob Blake; the Mustangs, coached by Frank Driscoll; and the Vikings, coached by Charlie Brewer. Each team had three divisions based on the ages of the players. (Charlie Brewer collection.)

The School Business Partnership, an initiative of then superintendent of schools Sam Leone in partnership with the East Hartford Chamber of Commerce, was established in 1990 to encourage local businesses to participate in programs with the school district. Mentoring, job shadowing, and internships, as well as the high school finance academy, are just a few of the successful programs that are a result of the partnership. Shown in 1994 are, from left to right, Rosemary Moynihan, Jackie Danise, Roy Spiller, George Drumm, Dan Coulom, and George Stewart. (Jackie Danise collection.)

Since the East Hartford Woman's Club was organized in 1954, this 95-plus-member organization has been dedicated to community service. A few of its significant contributions to the community include raising money for academic scholarships, providing financial assistance to four area high schools for Project Graduation, supporting the East Hartford Special Olympics, and gifting books to local school libraries. Pictured here in 1994 are members Gloria Juergens, Margaret Spiller, Ruth Sheehan, Debby Wood, Betty Ghagan, and Beverly Leone. (Jackie Danise collection.)

The East Hartford railroad station was located northwest of the underpass on Main Street. When it was decommissioned by the railroad, the building was rented to the Robinson Clay and Pipe Company, located on Tolland Street, and used for storage. At the time, clay pipes were packed in excelsior. One day, a Ford model A truck from the Robinson Clay and Pipe Company backed up to the building to unload a shipment. The truck got too close to the excelsior packing and ignited the building, which rapidly burned to the ground. (University of Connecticut, Thomas J. Dodd Research Center collection.)

The switchman's cabin was staffed by one or two men who were responsible for manually switching the tracks in the freight yard. The small handcar adjacent to the building would be used to inspect track conditions. The cabin and the switchman are fondly remembered by Bidwell Street resident Lou Morgan; when no trains were scheduled, the switchman would give him a ride to Manchester to visit his relatives. (University of Connecticut, Thomas J. Dodd Research Center collection.)

Two railroad stations once existed in town—the Main Street station and this one located in Burnside. The railroad first came to town in 1849 as the Hartford, Providence and Fishkill Railroad extended its tracks eastward from Hartford. Much of the construction work for the railroad was done by Irish immigrants. Many of these workers would later settle and raise families in the north end of town. (University of Connecticut, Thomas J. Dodd Research Center collection.)

Percy Spiller, Anna Generous, and Doris Spiller, from left to right, are ready to go for a pleasant buggy ride. Transportation by horse and wagon was rapidly becoming a thing of the past when this photograph was taken in 1925. (Roy Spiller collection.)

Warren G. Harding was president, and Babe Ruth was playing for the New York Yankees after the Red Sox had traded him for $125,000 two years earlier. A new Buick roadster could be purchased for $1,495, but Josiah C. Spiller and his horse Bess seem content to travel the old-fashioned way in this 1922 photograph. (Roy Spiller collection.)

East Hartford celebrated the end of World War II in 1945 with the whole nation. A huge parade was held on Main Street, and the Rotary Club's float proudly displayed the V for victory symbol, which was used by allies throughout the world. (Francis Hoffman family collection.)

This 1960s photograph shows the block on Main Street where Anderson Jewelers is located. Many other familiar town businesses are visible, including Pat's Medical Pharmacy, Berner and Sons Electrical Supplies, and Sherman's Men's Wear, which was known far and wide for its outstanding selection of neckties. (Agnelli family collection.)

Mayor John W. Shaughnessy Jr. cuts the ribbon for the opening of the Meadow Hill senior housing complex on September 3, 1966. The 10-story building would be administered and maintained by East Hartford Housing Authority members Rocco J. Alexander, Pasquale A. Fiorita, Stanley Ozimek, Frank Barone, Raymond St. Peter, and Eugene Sullivan. (Raymond Library collection.)

A huge parade was held in 1983 to celebrate the town's bicentennial. Proudly riding atop this 19th-century stagecoach is Robert P. Lynch, town resident and president of First Federal Savings. (Rebecca Lynch collection.)

The League of Women Voters called 1970 "the Year of the Voter" because of three anniversaries—the 50th anniversary of the League of Women Voters, the 50th year of women's suffrage, and the 100th anniversary of black suffrage. The East Hartford League of Women Voters sent two of its officers to the national convention in Washington that year—Mary Brennan (left), first vice president, and newly elected president Doris Suessman. (Raymond Library collection.)

Army Air Corps master sergeant Merton Pitkin and his wife Marjorie of Tolland Street visit town hall after his return from serving in the China-Burma-India Theater during World War II. Merton, who was employed at Pratt and Whitney, was a direct descendant of one of the founders of East Hartford. Pitkin family members still currently reside in town. As the cover of this 1945 town report aptly states, East Hartford was then, and still is, a good town to come home to. (Lois Pitkin Auclair collection.)

ABOUT THE EAST HARTFORD ROTARY CLUB

The East Hartford Rotary Club, charted in 1928, has long distinguished itself through community projects. Even a partial list would include the restoration of the Seldon Brewer House on Main Street; scoreboards at East Hartford High School, East Hartford Middle School, and McKenna Field; donations of a senior citizens' bus, a showmobile, and a music shell; the Eternal Light for Peace at the town library; and a gazebo on the town green.

In 1951, we established our scholarship trust, and since then we have awarded hundreds of thousands of dollars in scholarships to East Hartford's most promising young scholars. We were charter sponsors of the East Hartford Little League in the early 1950s; funded a community forum to plan for the future of East Hartford in 1993 and 1994; and have provided innumerable hours of volunteer support to the Special Olympics, the Greater Hartford Marathon, American Lung Association, and the East Hartford YMCA. Every Christmas we "ring the bell" in support of the Salvation Army. Continuing our emphasis on education, over the next two years Rotary has pledged $30,000 in support of the "Project Lead the Way" program, a new initiative that focuses on math, science, and engineering in the middle school and high school.

To cultivate the causes of peace and understanding across the globe, we have hosted and sponsored entrants in Rotary International Group Study Exchanges (young educators, professional, and business people) with such countries as Belgium, Australia, Argentina, England, France, South Korea, South Africa, Singapore, Sweden (Congressman John Larson), Brazil, Germany, and Norway, to mention a few. We have also hosted and sponsored high school exchange students from many of these same countries.

Rotary International projects have long claimed East Hartford Rotarian involvement. Our club has contributed almost $275,000 to the Rotary Foundation through projects and major gifts. As our town enters the 21st century, the East Hartford Rotary Club continues its commitment to the town, our country, and the global community.

Visit us at
arcadiapublishing.com